T0128896

THE
MILKWEED
MAN

THE MILKWEED MAN

BRADY RHOADES

THE MILKWEED MAN

iUniverse books may be ordered through booksellers or by contacting:

iUniverse
1663 Liberty Drive
Bloomington, IN 47403
www.iuniverse.com
1-800-Authors (1-800-288-4677)

ISBN: 978-1-5320-7341-0 (sc)
ISBN: 978-1-5320-7342-7 (e)

Library of Congress Control Number: 2019904593

Print information available on the last page.

iUniverse rev. date: 05/28/2019

CONTENTS

WEIGHT

Tank walked backwards into the bay, exaggerating his steps to keep from tripping over the fins. He tightened the mask, adjusted the spout. The tide swirled around his ankles, a pelican hovered overhead and he smelled fish-pee and French fries.

The beach was shaped like a horseshoe and dotted with colorful umbrellas. The children pointed and laughed. Frankie hurled a stone, Tye imitated Tank's walk and Gene, the most vicious of them all, lowered his head and glowered.

"Let's go," said Frankie, grabbing his fins.

Tye and Gene, nudging aside other boys, emerged with gear. Miss Ragland, the redheaded stick-figure long on grammatical etiquette and short on courage, outfitted the other children in fins, masks, spouts, and lathered them in sunscreen. Two slim-waisted high school boys in red shorts were more interested in slapfighting than lifeguarding.

Here came Crystal Betts, who made Tank so nervous his rectum tightened, and a few others. He could see Frankie and Tye and Gene sprinting to the water. Tank lowered his rump in the bath. The insults he'd heard so many times in the world he was dropping out of echoed in his head: *fatboy, tubby, lardass. Tank's so big his waist-size is equator.* He'd heard that one on the bus. Several girls had giggled and he'd smiled to mask his embarrassment. Even Miss Ragland called him Tank—though his name was Paul—because he wore a heavy green jacket whether it was twenty degrees or ninety eight, and he was short and wide, like an assault vehicle.

"Tank!" she waved. He couldn't tell if he was in trouble—he had drifted beyond the others, ignoring her rule—or if she was genuinely concerned. "Damnit," she said, pulling a pair of fins from the box.

Only his head showed; his eyes were like a crocodile's on the surface of *Bahia de Muertes*. He could see the histrionics on the beach and Frankie, Tye and Gene in the shallows of the bay, but as he sank into the depths the heads, along with Miss Ragland duck-walking to the sea, this field trip, the entire sixth grade of Jefferson Elementary School and all of the school's best intentions to shape the minds of five hundred children mattered less and less.

"He's too far out," said Tye, fumbling with his mask.

Frankie felt, for the first time, unathletic, and Gene, a violent swimmer, was having trouble trusting that he would not drift beyond the cove. The boys searched for Tank, who was twenty yards beyond the rest of the class, and not just snorkeling, but diving down, coming up for air minutes later, blowing his spout like a baby whale, floating on his back like an otter. He swam toward the beach, pretending to be a shark, convinced he could breath under water, homing in on the spindly, corpse-white legs of Gene, who, days before, had spat on him.

"Paff!"

Gene went under with a plunk, bobbed back up like a top, gasping for air, too frightened to scream, and was yanked back down.

Frankie and Tye swam to shore with a tenacity that panicked the other children. Miss Ragland had managed to lose a fin and was preoccupied with finding it. Gene came up and just as he shaped his mouth into a cry for help he was dunked with an assertive jerk. From the beach, John Mallumian, a bespectacled, straight-A student who refused to wear a swimsuit, figured Gene was overmatched.

"Shark!" he yelled, flapping his arms. "Shark!"

The children, waved in by Mallumian and the lifeguards, stumbled out of the water and onto the beach—Frankie, Tye, Crystal Betts, three crying cheerleaders, a gaggle of jocks, and Miss Ragland, straining to pull off a fin, snot oozing from a nostril, tried to take a head count.

"It's Gene!" Frankie said.

"Gene!" Miss Ragland repeated. "Gene!"

They looked out at the bay, which was lifeless and stayed that way for a long minute of curses, even prayers, before Gene's head appeared, his mask and snorkel askew, his mouth agape. They pulled him from the water and he splatted in the mud like a sopped fish, coughing up water, wheezing for air, as pale and green as iceberg lettuce.

"Give him room," said Miss Ragland, but the children did not move. They were as pale and green as Gene. They studied him for wounds, waited word of the shark, it's girth, the length of its teeth, the way it looked in the eyes, but Gene, as limp as seaweed, terrifically exhausted, mustering a singular charge of energy, lifted his head and choked out *Tank* before falling unconscious.

Tank had become porpoise-like, diving under for long spells, coming up to swallow enough air to go back down. He did not look around when he came up, nor did he search for a rock or boat on which to rest. From the beach, they saw him breach in an arc and spear down with a little splash. He could hold his breath for three minutes, dive twenty feet down and he was venturing beyond the cove, to the blue-green Sea of Cortez.

"What is he doing?" Miss Ragland was beside herself.

"Come back!" yelled the cheerleaders.

The boys were bested by anger, calling Tank "stupid," "idiot," "worthless," then disdain, shouting fat jokes they'd been shouting for years, noting that a family of whales had mistaken him for one of their own.

"He's happier now," said Frankie.

"He's with his mother," said Tye.

A slight and tidy boy named Sam—who'd always gone unseen—inched over to the circle and stepped inside.

"He's a fat bag of goo," he hissed.

Tank turned at the limpet-swarmed rocks on the north side of the cove, an instinctive fish swimming to the sun.

"He's not coming back," Mallumian said.

A lifeguard looked through binoculars. "I can't see him."

One of the cheerleaders sobbed.

Tank swam with yellowtail, batfish, snappers, tangs, grunts and a huge puffer—all different sizes, shapes and colors. He frolicked with clowns, teased a flounder, chased a marlin. The doe-eyed puffer followed him wherever he went.

He was training himself to stay under, until someday, he told himself, he would come up for air—an annoying distraction, and the sky was so cold it bit—just three times a day.

He had come from the sea, they all had, even Gene, lost soul, and he told himself that one day, in a million years, or two zillion, they would swim together, Frankies and goatfish and Tyes and eels and Genes and Crystals and seals and Miss Ragland, in a place where everyone feels weightless.

UNFINISHED MAN

Interruptions angled in.
"Life," he said, "is a series
of synaptic misfires, toward no finish."

It was this and that—a sickly cat,
unclean flue, verbose cousin,
taxes, busted pipes, weeds,

a conspiracy to tend to things,
but how do so
when stunned by existence?

In boyish moments,
beneath a tree in White Rock Canyon,
or on a sandy outfall by the lake,

he sensed he was tacking,
within himself,
to a new beginning.

Then, gray day, reading *Analects*
and pondering *imago dei,*
it came, as in a fever, an idea

of the world and his place in it,
and just as a thought blossomed
into words,

his father, who looked like God in bifocals,
peered up from a crossword and hollered
"Crackpot!"

MANDELL

At seventy, he said: "When the time comes, I want to
disappear like the Cheshire cat."
At eighty four: "It was easier when I was eighty."
At ninety, as family rallied
at Hoag Hospital, held his hands, prayed:
"Hope is not what's needed now."

Mandell, a tree of a man who's now a stick, hasn't
spoken since. The youngest son, the Didi of the tribe,
steals a moment with this host of
Lou Gehrig's disease and thinks:
What the F did he mean by that?

He could pore over the corpus of Mandell's life
and never know. He lets go,
takes a hit of Bushmills, dabs Mandell's lips,
tells a joke and Mandell's
out again with a little grin.

LETTER FROM A DEAD MAN WHO WAS UNCOMMONLY QUIET

Flies, I waved them off
but they boomeranged.
They loved me;
I loathed them.

Birds swooned in the sky
like fathers
of flies.

The people wished to fly too.
They hovered,
pecked, stung.

At night, when I sought solitude,
the phone rang,
a cat peered in,

car alarms, crickets,
hinges, wind,
all the pretty screaming.

Stranger, friend,

my life was not mine
and everyone knew it
but me.

THE LONGING LONGHAIR

I have lived on the lip
of insanity, wanting to know reasons,
knocking on a door. It opens.
I've been knocking from the inside!—Rumi

Look at the dog, digging, digging,
failing to break ground. His name
is Freckles, we're told, a little longhair

longing for the other side of the door.
Too short and no opposable thumb
so he plays to his strengths and wrecks

the floor. Because you can open
the door, you're God. Because he's here,
heaven's *out there*. A snack can't sate him,

nor a slow cat, though it would help for
a spell. It comes down to that goddamn
door, and all the humans are howling.

THE RECLUSE

        Therrre—
in.

He unskulls his hat,
frisbees it a-
        cross Apartment 8.
Nine hard hours shatter;
his brain begins to breathe.

His parrot, Maupassant, croaks:
"AskWhhhatMust I do? AnnndDoIt."

Miles west,
the unfinished face
of Ta Shunka-Witco
        rises o-
ver Pa Sapa.

He'd like to live
to see

the stone jaw, sigh for the holocaust
one final time,
and make his case
before the Custer Council.
You don't name a city after a wingnut.

Ta Shunka-Witco died on the floor
of the adjutant's office

in Fort Robinson, Nebraska
on Sept. 6, 1877,

one hundred forty one years ago—
injured by immigrants,
finished off by the tosspots of his tribe.

The recluse in No. 8
is wounded but alive.

He pours three fingers of Old Crow
with a beer chaser
and figures his finale.
Down Ghost Road go mother,
father, sisters, his sole friend.

Some focus, some flexations, occur.
He sings *Happy Deathday* with Maupassant,
spends six minutes on nostalgia,
smiling a hobo smile
at the 1990s.

The world's largest sculpture
cools on the Black Hills of South Dakota.

He sits at his desk
and writes his address
to the council
with the current lance
of the Sioux: a ballpoint pen.

'FREEDOM IS NOT WHAT WE THOUGHT'

The women smoke; the men smell like pork fat
and drink from paper bags.

A mile away, boys swim in the Dnipro rivermuck.
Two die for every one born here.

A man with a pocked face shakes my hand.
"I am Oleg. This is my wife, Galina."

Two years ago, in Independent Square:
"Ya Stoyav na Maidaimi!"

Now they miss the Cold War. "Freedom is not
what we thought." Could I spare some change?

Prosperity, peaceful sleep, justice…
It will not happen in their lifetimes.

Their hope is up ahead,
that way, far away.

We were the hope of our parents,
our parents the hope of theirs, so on,

through snapped shoelaces, sickness,
unnatural disasters, bad meat.

I'm waiting at a bus stop in Kyiv on a cold
August morning, to go to North Sea.

Oleg and Galina stand, a space
the size of a child between them.

DR. LINDQUIST

It's five hundred years from now. Changes in communication, commerce,
ways of thinking. The tattoo? As obsolete as Washington's wig.
Hip Hop? Zzzzz. Stephen Hawking's a crackpot.

Students find history a bore, but delight
in a profane scholar with a piebald scalp
who studies, for kicks, public bathrooms of the 21st century.

"Note the tissue, perforated in sections, the automated, weight-sensitive,
hands-off flushers. The sensory faucets, a flood-proof sprig for the palm,
no more! Air dryers, so they wouldn't go mad with towels."

Chuckles resound from the lecture hall. Hooting, paper tossing.
It's good to be the farthest point on the evolutionary line.
Who's more out-of-style than the dead?

"The Internet, smartphones, drones, AI, they're *part*
of the story," he says. "The johns round out The Age of Technology.
These people couldn't be trusted to shit properly."

THE EXPATRIATE

I.
The froth of the bay
comes laving over the city.
Trash and mud. Sea scum.
A smirking scat ray
kicked around the streets.

II.
What is it you say,
seven echoes from your birth?
You want a Japanese lover,
a parrot confidante?

III.
America's suicidal,
Europe's liquored up,
Baja's the crooked leg
of a woebegone dog.

IV.
Midnight,
relentless rain,
not a doctor in sight.
You are not the master
of your own shoes even.

V.
Devoured in La Paz
in the season of whales,
pity skin/grist/teeth,
praise what remains.

THE CABBIE

That your book? I asked, the third time through Hollywood.
Oh, that. I been askin' questions, and know what?
Schopenhauer makes nonsense. He can't say, you can't say, no one can.
God could if he would but he won't so it don't get said.
Tule, she stayed thin, at *fifty*. Do you know she fixed supper
if she was sad or glad or sick or whatever, and somethin' else,
she wasn't like these whores runnin' round, she was nice,
wore dresses to the end, smelled fresh,
damn pretty, 1940s-style, pretty and not stuck up.
Jesus Christ, never let a good woman go, they make life better.
The food's bad, Christmas stinks, the bird's irate.
I got no one, I got nothing. I don't pray to God no more
I pray to Tule but I'm gettin' the feelin' it's too late.

THE APE IN HIS CAGE

cleans his pelage.
                                        All night,
a ghoulish good time,
he pretended he was a person
pretending to be an outlaw ape,

thumped his chest, flashed his gums,
slow danced, drank beer, sobered up
at a teahouse in West L.A.
with a klatch of college gals
who said he made them laugh.

He played the role—a dude
in an ape suit sobering up
from a masquerade—glowingly,
crossing his legs, sipping chai,
grooming ladies for laughs.

It was good, though he needed
to masturbate, and itched fiercely,
to un-ape oneself for a night,
to be someone else,
though humans were a let-down.

It's Sunday morning at the zoo.
Jailed and free animals
take stock of one another,
the goats suspicious,
the old men erratic.

The middling primates,
dragging their knuckles,

competitive, brooding,
draw hordes of people
poised to unpeople.

The ape cleans his pelage.
The people—
one cried
on his arm just last night—press
their faces

against the bars of the cage,
scratch their backs,
hop up and down,
hoot and holler,
beat their chests and flash their gums.

BEAUTY DIED IN THE '40S

Mother stacks towels
the world was good once
it's all gone to shit

a small quick woman
she checks the tea
straightens Cezanne's
"Bend in the Road"

it's coming to an end
for the girl from Waterloo
no sense of decency

this is what old folks do
just as they're getting going
just as they've got it down
has everyone lost their mind?

she frets about the rain tree
planted after The Drought
of '98

too much
just say
beauty died in the '40s
ever seen Rita Hayworth?

not to mention the men
lean
groomed

people were kind
the world's gone mad
I'm glad I won't
be around to see it.

THE CABAZON

He'd been swimming in the soup
of Seal Beach,
sliding along and
something from above…

By the time
I saw him halfway down
the gut-stinking pier,
a Chicago bear had one

paw shoved down his mouth:
slishslosh slooosh.
The tatted bear—
51, 50, 54—

worked around the spikes,
pried open the
patient.
Useless, he said, tossing

his prey;
it face-planted on a rail,
fell forty feet and
we peeked…

He landed with a bouquet splash
inches from a seal's
open gob in the foreground
of the magniloquent mansions

on the high beach to the north.

THE SMITTEN SCIENTIST

The moon is waist deep in Lake Qinghai. You hear cloth pounding, horses
neighing.
Two hours ago you raised your glass of rice wine, gripped a chemist's arm
and toasted twilight over duck tongue soup.

You've seen cotton blossoms blowing in Beijing, the skyline of Shanghai,
but today it was silk makers reaching for your pants with ruined hands,
a little girl lugging pots of gruel and you, American, were lost.

You know about dynasties, rites of passage,
the grace and danger of bikes bursting like insects through a crossway,
the genius of a wok, the endurance of feet, the length of five thousand
years.

Never drink with a kind chemist pining for a Taiwanese shirtmaker.
Just when you think you know China, there's Mao, smug in the lamplight,
and Colonel Sanders has made his way to the cities.

TABASCO ESTADA, MEXICO, 1992

The cow—overeater, sad-sack napper—moped;
flies realized her pacifism.

All she wanted was tree-shade,
a patch of green, a patch of peace, across the road,

made eye contact with no one
(straight-ahead gaze, no trouble, thanks)

and a speeding jeep to the ribs
thrilled the birds in the leaves;

she folded up in sections,
out-clouded a Helenian moan and

the driver, a pressed, forward man, soothed the hood
and cursed her shattered there in the sun.

THOSE BABY BOOMERS WHO
LIVED FOR THE DAY

were happy very happy
lewdly airy
like the open fly

lolled
like peas
on buttered spoons

all they needed
was wine
whiskey
their gals
playlists
fish soup
the Baltimore Orioles

but it gets
to be a
gettin' havin' life

happy barely happy
who ponders
city lines
parking fines
the cost
of pork
the lure of a good roofer

welders
jockeys

cooks
teachers
pitchmen
public defenders
nurses on their smoke breaks

even braggarts
that have it all
that we can't stand

at all
happy rarely happy
must know

it gets
to be a
gettin' havin' life

MARCUS

Then disappointment, a thoughtless apercu, dragoons you
to the marrow...

We're a mile from the whet and scud of downtown,
in line for dinner and a cot.

His sneakers are clean, like surgical slippers,
his Angels shirt spotless.

We talk baseball.
"I'm tellin' you, man, it comes down to Madson's elbow."

The team led the league in blown saves last season,
so I can't object, but come on,

Out there in the rye, you've got Trout,
Pujols, Trumbo.

It's March 6. Opening Day is April 1.
"Burnett's an all-right set-up guy, but you gotta close," he says.

"Score all the runs you want, but ain't got a closer
them Rangers gonna run wild on ya'll."

"Where'd you play?" I ask.
"Wilson, then Long Beach State."

There are dozens of souls seeking
a soft spot to lie—itchy, cacophonous,

karma-mucked or just plain fucked
by The Great Recession.

"How long have you been on the streets?"
"Years." "What happened?" "Drugs, and no kinda luck."

"You got the first you got a good shot at the second," I say.
He's broad, corn-rowed; I count three teeth.

"You like your meth."
He grins. "My angel, my beast."

He starts again on the bullpen, how you gotta *save*
and I wonder: What was he born into, what ensued?

I do not know and do not ask.
It's anyone's guess.

"I dunno," he says. "You got the second
you got the first far's I can tell."

THE ROUGH-TIT CRAB

The news breaks in. Leslie Miller is poised and pretty
at a gas pump in Aliso Viejo. $2.89 a gallon.

There's a fire in Twin Pines. Trees are tipping over
and smoke blows north, shaped like Greek gods.

Six months since she left. I've been living on corn dogs
and beer (that's not a complaint).

Some days I'm ready to be wedded to oblivion;
others, I drink to sound sleepers, land owners.

Millions watch TV and believe if you work
hard enough, you get what you want.

Eduardo Alms explains the dangers of homegrown peas.
What hair, like a houseplant, and a tie with a gumball knot.

A rough-tit crab escapes a pot in Baltimore. He's six doors,
four gates, fourteen streets and a ramp from Chesapeake Bay.

He'll never make it, but don't tell him that, OK?

THE IDIOTIC PERSIFLAGE

Jack's, on the south side of Pittsburgh.
Clouds shake their beards
and leak on Carson Street.
A little-person runs across the bar,
cursing the crowd.

"I don't want to go home," says Ruth,
whom I've known since 9:30.
She's in a fight with her husband,
the historian, the tenured,
the fortunate and full-proof.

She's a broke lit-adjunct
so she has to listen
to him *za za za*
on the *Weirshact*.

She's past pretty, butchered from sarcoma
and thickened from drink.

Last call. Cazadores for me, gin for her.
"He called me an idiotic persiflage," she says,
"a drooling, elephantine hypocrite.
He talks that way."
She quotes *Love in the Time of Cholera*.

The little-man wears a Pens cap.
He's shirtless, holding a cup,
making the rounds for tips.
One guy sticks a buck in his waistband;
one last insult.

We leave. The streets are sippy, she says.
I'm tippling enough to flirt
with homicide on the historian,
It's closing time in the City of Bridges,
bridges to nowhere, everywhere.

More *Cholera*. "Go on," I say, taking her by
the elbow to the Roberto Clemente statue.

"Do you know it's the forty-year birthday
of his plane going down off Isla Verde?"
She smiles, mildly, her first of the night,
and we careen down Carson,
trying not to fall.

THE BATTLES OF ALESSANDRO

Dates: 1970-present.

Places: Konova, Erlanger, Batesville, Cincinnati, St. Louis,
Huntington Beach, Seal Beach, Las Vegas,
Frankfurt, Norwalk, classrooms, playgrounds,hospitals, St. James, St. Joseph's,
Bromly, Wintsville,
State Route 68, the Vincent Thomas Bridge.

Allies: Linda, Dad, Benny, Phillip, Lehigh, Bly the cat,
Joe Spencer, Dickie Gilbert, Jordan, Maridee, Miroslav Holub, Whitman,
Dickinson, Merwyn, Styron's *Darkness Visible,* Jean Cocteau, Bill Evans,
Ravel, Debussy, Satie, Van Morrison, Wayne Shorter, Miles Davis,
Charles Mingus, Stevie Wonder, Steely Dan, Sting, Hugh Masakela.

Foes: Syndactyly, cancer, biology, depression, nerves, noise, the 2 p.m.
yips, bridges, elevators, flagitious flocks.

Conflicts: The surgeries of '70-74, brawls at Lincoln Elementary, Bromly,
Wintsville, Gesler, ontological arguments at St. James and St. Joseph's,
the Panic Attack of '87, climbing from ditches in the '90s,
another saw-job in 2000, soldiering through interferon, through
Darvon addiction, the bankruptcy of '06, unemployment, PTSD.

Casualties: Grandpa Benny, Matt Clow, Dorothy, a mangled right hand,
lymph nodes, nerve damage in the shoulder, loss of muscle,
blood, treasure, both knees.

At issue: Genetics, sorrow, anxiety, the transgressions of the hordes, health,
injustice, state bullying, genetics, clerical harrowing, plain old rage,
the future, money, *goddamned genetics,* preservation of the Capitol Self.

Present status: Alessandro hunkers down in his Norwalk flat,
blinds shut, wife at work, drawing, playing guitar,
some portions in ruins, some crumbling, some standing somehow.

THE COWARD

When he came home from the war,
his wife lay with him,
fretting for his soul after all the killing.

He described camping, stew,
starlit nights on the plains.

"What about the… you know?" she asked.
"I didn't kill anyone," he said. "I mostly ducked."

He shared survival tricks: bury yourself in bodies,
get sick with flu, backpedal from the Rio Grande,
re-enter the fray when it's safe.

Confident in her arms, he grinned.
"What do I care? I *like* Mexicans."

She sat up. His head fell.
"What did you say?"

"I love life," he said. "The stars, smells, making love—"
"How could you? How about duty, honor?"
"It's not true," he said. "They're not worth dying for."

He prattled on—a peaceful, pauper's life under Mexican rule,
sweeping, cooking, "making love to you"

but she was gone, into the night
and he watched from a window, for a little while.

THE CHIMP WHO WOULD BE KING

I.
A boy was born into privilege.
His family spared nothing
for his comfort,
taught him with luxury
comes duty; theirs
was a history of statesmen and lords.
"You shall be statesman or lord," they said,
and he, in his little sweater, nodded.
He was an agreeable child
though thirty three percent chimp.

II.
"Pan Troglodytes," the doctor said,
adding he had seen one other case;
the man-chimp was a clerk,
owned a home in the savannah.
The boy-chimp had sad eyes, large hands,
a black back, a mischievous disposition.
He refused milk, preferring to feed on
fruits, seeds, the occasional bush pig.
He sulked on the roof. He learned to read
a little when he was twelve years old.

III.
His folks were unfazed.
They assigned him tutors,
removed hair from his nape and palms,
corrected his charmingly gummy smile,
and taught him not to holler, climb things,
walk on his knuckles, groom friends.
They forbade the word "chimp"

under any and all circumstances.
"The thing to do," his father said, "is focus
on his strengths."

IV.
The boy-chimp attended elite schools
on legacy waivers.
He excelled in gymnastics.
"A late bloomer," the parents said.
After college, he bankrupted a business.
"Bad timing," they said, blaming the market,
and it was "stress, growing pains,
a child's misguided soul"
that caused him to drink all those
banana rums.

V.
He ran for a province post—and won.
His father surrounded him with aides
instructed to translate issues
into terms he could comprehend,
and to never let him read in public.
They honed an image of a stern
taskmaster who used catchphrases like
"Get after it" and "Don't think it to death,"
a delegator who left the minutia
to bookworms and policy wonks.

VI.
The treatments worked; his spine straightened,
and doctors removed the back brace.
He'd stopped drinking,
hadn't hopped on a counter in years,
and rarely, in public,
did he comb through the heads of pals.
He was reading more. A staffer,

after much balking, convinced him to try
Kipling's "The Jungle," which he adored.
"He can be lord," his father said.

VII.
The man-chimp ran for lordship.
Tycoons paid for his campaign.
There were rumors that he was dumb,
"Dumb as a chimpanzee," his foes said.
He responded by telling voters
he would get rid of all the bad guys.
He had excelled at that in the province,
reviewing cases for ten minutes—
the small font angered him—
before signing off on executions.

VIII.
It cost heaps of money,
but he was named lord.
He was surrounded by scholars
who did most of his reading for him.
He struggled. The press was rough,
and world leaders spoke strange languages.
He choked on a cracker and passed out
while wrestling with his dogs.
There were sessions at sunrise; he was taught,
for instance, "gross national product."

VIIII.
Then the land was attacked.
He knew exactly what to do.
"I'll get rid of all the bad guys," he said.
It was obvious. Who could argue?
He galloped and hollered through the castle.
He swung from a chandelier.
He threw feces at a cook.

"I'll get rid of 'em!" he told the nation.
"I'll get rid of the bad guys
and the world will be a gooder place."

*Note: This story, both fantastical and troubling, was dismissed in its time,
revived later as a joke, then fable, before gaining credibility
as a work of journalism borne out by the facts.*

*Note No. 2: The man-chimp flattened countries, killed tens of thousands,
wounded hundreds of thousands, but failed in his objective.
There are still bad guys.*

MOTHER, 2013

Beneath the huge homes
and hulking oaks of Claraboya,
she fades in her modest room in Claremont, California.

Each morning she shined the mausoleum of my youth:

Mt. Baldy, Frisbee, father
in the garage, digging through nails,
and she made him feel manly at ten-grand a year,

told her kids, in our JC Penney shoes, we were going places,

she of the love too great to reciprocate,
from a threadbare tent
on the Arkansas River,

padding over the mule tracks of The Depression,

and now, an autumn Monday after the rains,
the skyline rises to the waist of the sun
and all turns golden for a moment.

FATHER, 1975

He's in the garage, cursing a '66 Mustang
with 200,000 on her.
Someone drove her cross-country too much;
the sod of Middle America
clings like fungus to the wheel-wells;
the engine wheezes.

He's a mechanic's son from South Bend
whose politics can be summed up
as pro little guy. He likes the garage,
where he can right wrongs, take a
no-hope Ford and make her run again.
He's been greasy and bleeding for weeks.

We emerge on a Sunday morning—
she's humming, man—and cut off
a Mercedes-Benz 6.9. The driver flips
the bird and my Dad cracks up.
"Always cut off these fancy asses,
they got more to lose than we do."

ASI PASA LA VITA

I'm goin' with a white ruffle top with wide leg jeans I shred against
everyone's blah blah. *Please.* Guys don't know style.
A little leg never hurt, heels that jack me from 5-3 to 5-7.
Dangly earrings. Nude lipstick. Mani, pedi, *oh yeah.* All goes
to the eyes; mine are big and warm. One guy said *cloying.*

Twenty til he knocks, enters and tries. To. Keep. Entering. Sorry, it's true!
I like older boys. They know what work is, plus they're thankful.
Is he gonna speak in tongues? *Up to me.*
I read history, bios. Men are my specialty. *I know where they live.*
It's a moony night in La Puente, 70, smells like weed.

I'm 18 today, body to the bling boys. It's been like that since 8.
They call me *guarra,* they do, girls to my face, boys to boys.
Older boys are less mean, less drunk, less stinky.
My step-pop's in his chair, stroked out. Mama's blazin' on the stoop,
all *repararo,* back to her vows, but this girl don't spend time on iodine.

I bet he offers roses, a donut. Do I put him through confession?
*What do you hate about your looks? What's your idea of happines*s?
More vino. Maybe you think I'm lacksadaisical; my cells are
busy with salvation. They're gettin' saved. *In this temple.*
Asi pasa la vita. I'm church for congregation; enter me for ecstasy.

DIRTY OLD DOLL

You'd said so yourself
and now spoke out loud, outdoors,
where only prairie voles
could hear.
Fuckit.

The word did not apply to
those younger than fifty.
You were fifty five, did
what you were supposed to do
and sometimes what you wanted

but too much of the former and… *Vince.*
Any man who wears the same mustache
for thirty years—Hitleresque if you trimmed
a half-inch from either side—is anorak
to a fault.

You wanted a goatee, a beard,
something. He didn't even try
for romance, plus too much talk
of the chamber of commerce
and not enough

Duino Elegies.
"Ay, is night more easy
on lovers? Ay, they hide
their fate from themselves
by using each other."

Three weeks ago, you unhid
like a reckless, limping

hirsute in daylight,
drove (anywhere!),
arrived here.

Look at the sweet ovine faces
of sheep,
which remind you
of yourself
twenty years ago.

Vince's mustache endures,
like a natural law.
All your friends and family
will live and die
confused or delusional.

You don't apologize; you read
your private
poems to the holm oaks.
Four judder; the wind flings
and scatters your songs,

there's no rhyme or reason
to any of this, we sense.
The life you lived
is a broken plaything,
a dirty old doll.

You've gone homicidal
on homeostasis.
You watch prairie voles
and prairie voles
watch you

save one from the pack,
mechanospiritual?
You're thinking
this was meant to be,
free of constituency.

THE PRIEST

Whatever you can do, or dream you can, begin it. Boldness has genius,
power and magic in it—Goethe

For days it rained, the streets
are damp and gray, like a whale's back,
a paca-paca bird dries in the sun,
a priest, done diddling, looks out a window.

All is clean, calm, comely. Lima, with its gardens
and architecture, its wet, sexual hair
high in the trees and down in the grass,
looks and smells like a woman.

The priest dresses, from stiff collar to gleaming shoes,
parts his hair with a red comb and brews some joe.
Today is the day to stand a low man
before the flock and state,

"Here is a man, yeahyeah, here is a man,"
play mandolin, promise to guard the silent,
the suffering, and call for kindness,
for weeds, beetles, even Steven.

PHOTO OF AN AMERICAN ICON
AND HIS WIFE IN A CARE UNIT

Lying there in bed, in gown,
all the rues of love and loss
amassed beneath the eyes,
she's aged ten years in ten days
from a nervous bust-down
brought on, in part,
by her husband's stunts.

It's 1925.

Time passed or ran in laps,
what's it matter now?
Babe Ruth, who will clock
seven hundred homers
on his way to Cooperstown,
slumps bedside,
the weight of his thoughts in his hands.

UNCLE PATRICK

We've come to the jetty, after a wake for his wife,
to summon the Furies. A fisherman gathers line lengths
from his reel, a cormorant sleeps in a scoop of granite.

I'm thirteen; tissues flap from the nicks in my neck
and he tells a tale: Cronus taking a blade to Uranus,
a rusty shower falling, quenching some eternal thirst in the sea,

and there's Tisiphene, Allecto, Maguera, all their sisters since,
especially Jan—fierce, forgiving, divine.
I finger my cuts and the debris of county folk—

bottles, bags, a hankie—rocks to the rhythm of the tides;
he slides a flask from his vest and grins:
I'm gonna have a drink. You stand there and bleed awhile.

THE SWEEPER

sweeps the streets of Mumbai. It's a foggy dawn;
there's blood and hair on the stoop of a salon.
Garbage piles up in gutters.
Cancer patients spoon the walls of Tate Hospital;
there's Deepali Dahale with a clot in her eye.
One hopes she lives

to see her dowry.
The sweeper toes the remains
of a row involving two rupees.
The fog gets bored with itself.
Lights switch on.
There's movement in the streets.

NICK, NEIL, BRIT AND SUCH

"We are the beautiful too many"—Greg Brown

Late May in the foothills of the San Gabriel Mountains
7:15 p.m.
the valley
lights up
street to street
room to room
dusk darkens &
so goes
the burn for…

You hear
coyotes
crows
toads
taxpayers
feeding & fed
forging & filled
any old way

rivers
pour past
pines
willows
psychedelic
wilds

bumpbump
go
bushtits
siskins

cowbirds
phoebes
foxes
moles
gophers

hurried
harried
hallowed

OK
say it
blooming

also
beauty

these are kooky times

in *GirlsGirlsGirls*
two miles east
on Mills Way &
in the woods
sea depths
deserts
on Mt. Wilson
Mt. Baldy
the Himalayas

don't think
doomed

no
no

it's late May in the foothills
7:30 p.m.

a man
mounts his
homemade
pie
a stoned
childless
porch-bound
wife
thumb-loves
herself
as Lee
hose in hand
ogles from
the evergreen

those hope-doped
spawn

robust
colored
up

off to
prom
they
go

to
college
they
go

to
work

Nick
Neil
Brit &
such

go
go

it's late May
7:50 p.m.

the learning begins
in Autumn

DOROTHY

At McConnell's, she tore napkins into bits,
downed champagne, zinged a braggart,
asked for ice to chew on, slap-giggled her way
through a Hibbing tale gone bad,
worse than bad, a horror house, past sad.

She was fifty seven, gladly-widowed, cancer free,
dressed in black, and rainbow flip-flops,
a citizen, in her dream, of Mt. Paektu,
cubed from the cutting, better looking than Pablo's women

and—blink—scattered in the sage scrub
at Pelican Point, off on a breeze to sea,
The eulogist got the facts right but sold her short.
What can be said that was not in the obits?
She lived on Mt. Paektu, cubed, good-looking, it's true.

KEITH

We will never be complete in anything,
not awake or at rest,
but in-between, though we can't be placed exactly.

Did you ever love without a way out on the sly?
The days felt crepuscular
and I fell out of love with myself when I was just four.

Look, the corpse-clotted hill is loud
with Monday morning insults, bees tremble in glee.
   Friend,

we will always be part-this, part-that,
effete in our flower-stinking graves,
or in times like this, alive.

HOPE INCARNATE

Mother,
you are no more dead
than on your
last day,
as alive as on
your best day, 1974?
Forty years before your
ghost voyage…

That was apparition;
I see you
in the non-fiction
of my dreams.

At supper, there's beef,
green beans, rolls,
the floors gleam,
the war's over,
Dad got tenure,
your babies are safe,
you're wearing
a red-wrap dress.

After grace, you fix
my sleeve
and beam;
I'm hope incarnate.

Mother,
that's a funny,
hide-and-seek
game
you played
on Jan. 2, 2014.
I'll see you tonight
in your red dress, OK?

SLEEPLESS, BIPOLAR

Exactly—my father's stock response

Midnight; he's smoking, sculpting.
"The problem is all in your head."

He's heard that about
four thousand six hundred and eight times.

He has a cataleptic one, a great thing
come down the pike.

He lies down; it shuttles off,
glazed in interplanetary dust,

to a gourd light years
from Claremont, California.

He sips tea with a droll kink in his grin;
it bowls for war limbs with coconuts.

2:12 a.m. "It's in your head." He's heard that
four thousand six hundred and nine times.

That immense eight-ball,
using the neck for a cane,
walks him through the streets of the city.

GRANDFATHER, 1947

He shouldn't have married, they say,
but when he thought about it,
too late,
like a knot in his shoe.

A curious guy, mind adrift,
too good-looking
for his own good, the story goes.

What makes a man with no means put his nose
in a map every Sunday night and
drink a jug of wine by the train tracks
in his go-to chair?

His brother: "Every third Robbins gets the bad blood."
Not knowing the genealogical gist,
we leave it at that.

Summer in a South Bend park, 1941.
Mother plays tag;
Uncle Jimmy runs for trouble;
James tips his porkpie

over his eyes,
dozes to the Cubs on the radio,
and you wonder what he dreams of.

A DAY IN THE LIFE OF GODSE GOPAL

The Child
Godse wakes, naked, with jellied bowels from bad dreams,
unsure he can do it. The day, that is.
Dawn, like flashlights, creeps through wood slats.
He's quivering, eyes bloodshot, no time to sort out
the prior, pestilential hours. Off to work with tankards to ease
him into morning: 1) Pinot; 2) Water spiked with Listerine.

The Professional
At his desk, glasses on for the DL,
hearty greetings, a brisk walk,
a few phone calls, donuts for Laurie in HR.
Movement gains him mercy
for seven hours.
Mr. Gopal is a medical coder at Kaiser Hospital.

The Patient
The doc's 4 p.m. is trick-or-treating. "Some decent days,
some rough ones, the Klono evens me out, but without sleep…"
Here come the scripts. *Score.* Wine gets him through a.m.,
Klono through early p.m., Ambien through nights.
His *terminus ad quem* is the most constant thing:
to not end up in a ward like his dad, aunts, uncles.

The Artist
Dusk. A room in Anselmo, Nebraska.
He got past his landlord,
and on to Gogol, Milosz, his muted horn,
a news report on native tribes and foul water.
He feels like a tag-sale trinket
prized for its weirdness, thirty three years later.

The Historian
Time for an Irish Exit to the barn.
"I write from a hole in the haymow I dug."
His book is long, too long.
He enturtles his head, sleeps with a note in his ear.
His heart is a drum.
The note reads, "The performance is over."

THE VETERAN

2:10 p.m., June 6, 2009, one month to the hour Pops died.
He saw a baby the same day.

Pops, privates showing, gums itching, moody,
was a diseased infant.

The infant he'd homed in on and named Vo Minh?
An old man undawned upon.

He did what dying men and doomed babies do: napped, shat,
and what they don't: jerked off, shadow boxed, ate biscuits.

Kien Hoa is now known as Ben Tre. He does not dress, nor care.
Sitting in a glider chair, he laughs in his good hand.

CORPORATE CASUALTIES

drinking at a bar in Long Beach
6 weeks after
the company
laid off
35
there's 1
hey
hey
I buy him a rum & coke
any prospects?
looks
calls
makes his pitch
52
2 decades on the job
200 sick days
unused
heard anything? could you put a word in?
no & yes
1 drink only
& he'd like to get the tip please
more perplexed
than pissed off
20 more days & he loses the house.

MEDICATED KYM

My neighbor's wailing
like a mother at her boy's wake.

I try to ignore but she's at the door,
left her meds in a cab the night before,

coming home from ER, so off we go and
she slurs, sleeps, nodding, waking and

she's got a law degree, wanted to be a judge,
uses words like *propulsive,* says about me:

"Currrozty zeemsshu be ur overrr i deng proc livteee."
The Mormons did a number on her,

the homophobes, and pile-ons:
neuropathy, arthritis, Lyme Disease.

What do you say to those in their penalty boxes?
We see a hippie holding a sign:

"Jesus said you must be born again."
Kym's fifty six, a rock collector,

floutist, city stroller,
a handsome woman humbled…

"You must be born again," I say. "Ha!" she laughs.
"I nahvr az shu be burn in za verst plaze…"

THE UNEMPLOYED SCHOLAR

Porch-muck rising in the flurry
of a corn rag,
a pontoon plane flopping on a pond,
the girding of Suez Bridge,
a gnat maddened by heat,

the contemplation of Rafah.

Neither Jean-Jacque Sempe
nor Ovid's poems
can sweep his mind clean and
there goes a tern
to the lost nation of Dzhan.

THE MILKWEED MAN

At 35, he made 50K a year,
at 40, more, at 44, much more.
It wasn't enough,
he was 10K away, always,
and sleep-deprived.

The more he made, the more he was,
the less, the less.
Commercials said so, folks acted as though.
He was Liszt,
competing against the world,

and in came Adrienne Rich:
My nerves sang the immense
fragility of all this sweetness
the green world already
sentimentalized, photographed, advertised to death.

2:18 a.m. There are
skeins of wooly pod milkweed
in the meadow—
who can resist?
It healed the Ohlones, the Choctaws.

Young man, young woman,
don't get The Milkweed Man
wrong.
Nobody questions
your lack of wooly pod

but money matters,
it pays rent, mortgage,

car loan,
credit card bills,
gives you security.

In four hours, he's off
to earn more,
pay off his truck—a yeoman
with a back ache
(that's what it takes).

They'll tell you to earn,
urge you to yearn.
Too much of the latter
and you're walking the streets
a little low, a little high,

dogs hoarse from moaning.
They're yearning, too.
They sound like you feel
but a little
less free.

It doesn't have to be.
Fill in what you must do
here _____.
Money matters;
you decide the price.

AA WHALE WATCHING TRIP

A skein of snow
falls from Mt. Antonio,

rain falls,
streams, rivers, fall,

seeds fall from phoebes,
to bracken and broom,

lovers to the waist
of desire,

seabirds and senior citizens
from struggle,

politicians from drowsy integrity,
into monied sleep.

In the capital, freedom falls
into fascism's arms,

present falls to past
and leaves

something new
to live up to

for the wrecked and ragged
on a cold boat

in a Baja lagoon,
and calves fall

from their mamas
and forge north.

THAT TWITCHY, AMBITIOUS, GODDAMNABLE NUB

H ome from jail, the first order of business was getting back his 10-bore shotgun. He called the Wrightwood Police Station.

"I want my gun."

"That's not up to me," a clerk said.

"Who's it up to?"

"The judge."

The clerk told him that because he faced charges of recklessly discharging a weapon, the gun would be confiscated until a judge made a ruling, and if he was found guilty, it could be taken away for good.

"No guarantee you'll get it back," she said.

"I shot birdseed," he said.

"Doesn't matter," the clerk said.

"I pointed it so's no one would get hurt."

"See the judge about your weapon, sir."

Big Jim hated the word *weapon*. The police had said it the night before and that had upset him. He had never shot anybody, he told them, but they didn't care. He admitted to being drunk and that had made his logic worthless as they took him away.

He walked from his trailer to the mailbox expecting more bad news— bills, probably. A neighbor eyed him while watering a plant.

"You woke me last night."

"Sorry about that."

In the distance, Arrowhead Mountain was shedding the last of the winter snows and turning blue-green against a startling sky. Spring was coming, meaning Big Jim's mother would visit, and seeing her labored walk, he would be reminded of his father.

He opened the mailbox, gathered the mail, and an object in the back of the box caught his eye.

"Jesus!" He dropped it, hopped back, bent over to get a closer look. "Jesus."

It was a thumb with an ingrown nail and hairy knuckle, a hardworking thumb, crooked, banged up. It might have been turning pale green; he wasn't sure. There were dollops of dried blood on the ground. He slipped the digit into his pocket and followed the trail. He did not call the police because he was angry at them for keeping his gun.

He wove around the clubhouse, in and out of alleyways, across Main Way and back several times, arriving at a doorstep on the other side of the park.

The trailer looked like most of the other trailers: in need of a paint job, browning plants lining the exterior, an unwashed truck in the parking spot. He pulled the thumb from his pocket and matched it to his own. His was bigger. He knocked on the door.

Someone uttered something.

He knocked again, louder.

"Whaddya want?"

"Got something!"

Jim turned the doorknob and peered in. A wiry, shirtless man with a pig's nose sat on a couch with a handgun on his thigh. The handgun looked to be a single-action Army revolver. The man's left hand was wrapped in a blood-soaked towel. On the coffee table lay a knife, a pen and a sheet of blood-stained paper.

"What the fuck do you want?"

He held up the thumb. "I followed the trail."

"Good on you."

"Yours?"

"Yeah."

"Jesus."

"Don't matter."

"It don't seem—"

"I shot my wife, OK? Felt bad about it."

Jim wondered why he hadn't cut off his index finger. He glanced at the bedroom.

"Go and see for yourself."

He took two steps toward the door of the bedroom and saw her reflection in a mirror, slumped on the bed, heart spilling into her lap.

"Jesus Christ."

"She changed her mind. You don't change your mind."

"You couldn't talk ab—"

"She don't talk. Just cries and screams."

"You got her good. Want it back?" He held up the thumb.

"Nope."

The man began to write, looked up and asked, "What happened to your eye?"

"Got into it with the cops."

The man studied Jim, who was a shade over six-feet-two, square shouldered, with thick forearms. He was a drinker, you could tell that by the purple face, and a smoker: a box of Kents bulged from his sock.

"That was you?"

"My job pissed me off so I blew off some steam."

The man shifted his weight, which jarred his hand. He grimaced and fixed the wrapping.

"Guess you were my decoy then."

"What do you got so far?" Jim asked.

"I'm sorry."

Jim found out the man's name was Jeff, that he was from upstate New York and worked at a carpet store. In the room were a couch, a table, a wicker chair and a bookcase with fewer than ten books, one titled "Overcoming Anger."

"I've always had a lot of trouble with my temper," Jeff said.

"I got that problem," Jim said, sitting in the wicker chair.

Jeff hurt other people when he got mad; Jim hurt himself, mainly. Either way, it was bad. All of the violence had been really bad.

"I think that'll do the trick," Jeff said.

The note read:

I'm sorry for what I did. I could not control myself after she changed her mind. I never could control myself. It is better if I go.

Jeff

Jim rose.

"You mind calling the cops?" Jeff asked.

"Not at all."

"And don't give 'em my thumb?"

Jim paused.

"They don't need it," Jeff said.

Halfway across the park, Jim heard a *poo-wa,* and looky-loos emerged from their homes. The boys made their hands into guns and blasted each other. The girls conversed in little cliques. A siren whined in the distance.

He walked from the park and kept walking, pondering what to do with the thumb. He could bury it, he thought, give it to a cat, stomp it to pieces…

He entered the First United Presbyterian Church nestled in the pines not far from the park, slid along the benches, kneeled and hung his head.

He said a prayer for Jeff and for Jeff's wife. He prayed for his mother and her bad hips, and bargained to get his gun back. The thumb, which he held with focused care, as if it were a sacred artifact, seemed to enlarge in his mind.

So much had been done by it: tool making, knife making, gun making, modern engineering. It was the opposable thumb that revolutionized war among the ancients, allowing them to hold spears and heave them at their foes from a safe distance; zealots used the thumb to ignite their torches in the Middle Ages; the battles of 18th century New Jersey, of Gettysburg, of The Bulge, of Hiroshima, of Iraq and Afghanistan, all, to some degree, hinged on the strength and steadiness of the thumb; the planes that sped like torpedoes into the Twin Towers—gripped at the wheel by that twitchy, ambitious, goddamnable nub; and the tragedy of tragedies, the thumb of his father hooked around a rope that lashed his mother's waist and made her walk lopsided.

Shadows slanted down from the San Bernardino Mountains, darkening the village. Jim sat on the steps of the church, staring at the wrinkles on the knuckle, which reminded him of his father, his grandfather, history, mankind. He almost laughed. He almost cried.

Printed in the United States
By Bookmasters